AF143892

BOOK ANALYSIS

Written by Vincent Guillaume and Gilles Clamar
Translated by Rebecca Neal

Against Nature

BY JORIS-KARL HUYSMANS

JORIS-KARL HUYSMANS

FRENCH WRITER AND ART CRITIC

- **Born in Paris in 1848.**
- **Died in Paris in 1907.**
- **Notable works:**
  - *Parisian Sketches* (1880), collection of prose writings
  - *Là-bas* (1891), novel
  - *The Cathedral* (1898), novel

The writer and art critic Charles-Marie-Georges Huysmans, better known under his pseudonym Joris-Karl Huysmans, was born in 1848 to a Dutch father and a French mother. At the start of his career, he was an admirer of Émile Zola (French writer and journalist, 1840-1902) and subscribed to the naturalist movement that Zola led, before moving away from this literary school with the publication of *Against Nature* in 1884. Throughout his life, he was part of the artistic avant-garde and constantly pushed boundaries with his writing.

In spite of his undeniable talent, Huysmans was a tormented individual who shunned society and politics and lived as an outcast. He was deeply misogynistic and the idea of reproduction repulsed him. His only real interests were art and religion: religion is a recurring theme in his work, and is central to the final third of his writing. For much of his life, he was agnostic and dabbled in mysticism and the occult, before seemingly finding the answers he was searching for with his conversion to Catholicism.

AGAINST NATURE

AN ANTINOVEL OF THE DECADENT MOVEMENT

- **Genre:** novel
- **Reference edition:** Huysmans, J-K. (2008) *Against Nature.* Trans. King, B. Sawtry: Dedalus.
- **1st edition:** 1884
- **Themes:** the Decadent Movement, boredom, loneliness, despair, idealism, art, literature

À rebours, which is generally translated as *Against Nature* or *Against the Grain* in English and was first published in 1884, is unique among Huysmans' works and marked a turning point in his literary career. Although its commercial success was initially limited, the author's contemporaries immediately recognised its brilliance and it is now considered a key work of French literature.

Huysmans' reputation largely rests on this novel, which could more accurately be described as an antinovel as it has virtually no plot. It centres on the Duc des Esseintes, an apathetic, misan-thropic, eccentric aristocrat with unusual tastes and habits. He hates and rejects all rules and deliberately isolates himself from society, which eventually results in him becoming unbearably neurotic.

SUMMARY

NOTICE

The Notice provides an account of the youth of the novel's protagonist, Duc Jean Floressas des Esseintes. This effeminate young man is the last descendent of an aristocratic family which has been declining for generations due to a series of consanguineous marriages. The narrator describes him as a sickly child who receives a "convivial and [...] pleasant" education with the Jesuits before turning to debauchery as a young adult, which leaves him prematurely exhausted. In the course of his education, he develops an "untamed intelligence", as well as an inclination to question and challenge the established order. When his parents die, they leave him a sizeable fortune, which he begins to squander as soon as he comes of age. After finishing school, he mixes with both young people of his own age and background and intellectuals, but soon finds himself disgusted with their pious obedience, meaningless debauchery, mundane conversations and greed. Before long, he is so tired of other people and feels so much contempt for humankind and society that he sells the family property and moves to "a secluded location with no neighbours", taking care not to give his new address to anyone.

CHAPTER I

The narrator describes some of des Esseintes' past eccentricities, such as the lavish meal he organised to celebrate becoming impotent: "A farewell dinner for a temporarily dead virility". He has now fully rejected society and chosen to live a comfortable, solitary life away from Paris. He decorates his new home tastefully, taking care to use colours that will suit his nocturnal lifestyle and look good under artificial lighting, and meticulously selecting his furniture.

CHAPTER II

Des Esseintes makes arrangements so that his two servants, who also worked in the castle where he grew up, will disturb him as little as possible. For example, he sets fixed times and seasonal menus for his frugal meals. He has furnished his dining room to look like the cabin of a boat, which reflects the fact that he prefers to travel in his imagination rather than in real life: "In short, artifice seemed to des Esseintes to be the distinctive stamp of man's genius".

CHAPTER III

The narrator outlines des Esseintes' tastes in Latin literature. He is not fond of classic authors such as Cicero (c. 102-43 BCE), Virgil (70-19 BCE), Horace (65-8 BCE) and Ovid (43 BCE-17/18 CE) because he sees their style as "debilitated", predictable and pompous. He prefers decadent works, such as the Satyricon (1st century CE) by Petronius (Latin writer, satirist and poet, died in 66 CE), the Christian literature of the 4th to 9th centuries and the works of a number of obscure authors who wrote in a corrupted form of Latin.

CHAPTER IV

In order to better show off an Eastern rug, des Esseintes has acquired a tortoise, painted it gold and studded its shell with jewels. When the tortoise is placed on the rug, its movements make the colours appear more vivid. After admiring his handiwork, he pours himself some whisky using his "mouth organ", an ingenious device that allows numerous spirits to be poured at once. Later on, when the sudden resurgence of a painful memory leaves him reeling, he looks for the tortoise to lift his spirits, but finds it dead in its bedazzled shell.

CHAPTER V

We are told that des Esseintes prefers paintings that depict dreams and imaginary scenes, in stark contrast to the realistic paintings that were popular at the time. In particular, he likes the tortured drawings of Jan Luyken (Dutch poet, illustrator, engraver and historical painter, 1649-1712) and Rodolphe Bresdin (French draughtsman and engraver, 1822-1885), the fascinating depictions of *Salome* (1876) by Gustave Moreau (French painter, 1826-1898) and the fantastic paintings of Odilon Redon (French painter and engraver, 1840-1916). Although numerous paintings adorn the walls of his sumptuously decorated bedroom, it is nevertheless reminiscent of a monk's cell, which symbolises his retreat from society.

CHAPTER VI

Des Esseintes reminisces about the pleasure he has derived from perversity, such as the time he corrupted a poor 16-year-old boy by bringing him into a wealthy household. His aim was to get the boy used to material comfort so that he would then be prepared to kill to feed his addiction to luxury, thus turning him into a danger to society.

CHAPTER VII

Des Esseintes is overwhelmed by memories and recalls his time with the Jesuits, where the Fathers treated the pupils as intellectual equals, while also constantly indulging their childish whims. He is sceptical and nonconformist by nature, which means that he never accepted the Jesuits' religious teachings during his schooling. By contrast, his isolation has inspired some stirrings of faith in him, but he knows that he is too rational and insufficiently humble to ever become a true believer. The feeling persists in spite of his efforts to shake it off, so he gives himself over to reflections on "the nothingness of existence" and contrasts the ideas of Schopenhauer

(German philosopher, 1788-1860) with the teachings of Catholicism, before throwing himself into decorating his home.

CHAPTER VIII

After first having his heart set on tropical flowers, then on artificial flowers, des Esseintes eventually acquires a collection of hairy, veiny, cankerous and carnivorous plants which are real but look fake. He is thrilled with his purchases, but the process of buying them has left him exhausted and they seem to be weighing down the atmosphere in his home. This inspires a nightmare in which syphilis is pursuing him on horseback.

CHAPTER IX

Des Esseintes has more and more nightmares, and the first physical signs of his neurosis begin to set in. He reads novels by Charles Dickens (English novelist, 1812-1870) in an attempt to calm down, but their prudishness proves counterproductive, and he is plunged into a series of memories steeped in lust. He recalls his past relationships with an androgynous female acrobat who looked like a man, a ventriloquist and a shy young man.

CHAPTER X

Des Esseintes is beset by olfactory hallucinations and starts smelling frangipane everywhere. He uses perfume to try and get rid of the smell. According to him, scent has its own language comparable to that of the spoken word, and each smell has its own meaning, which means that the history of perfumery is comparable to the history of literature. He himself is an expert in perfumery and begins preparing new concoctions with the same creative zeal as a writer. However, he is soon forced to abandon this pursuit because of violent headaches.

CHAPTER XI

Des Esseintes begins to feel stifled by his solitude and wants to travel to London. The gloomy weather in Paris helps him to imagine that he is already there. The illusion grows stronger when he goes to a tavern and tucks into a substantial meal of British food. He then recalls a disappointing trip to the Netherlands and decides against going to London, as he thinks that he has already seen everything he wanted to see.

CHAPTER XII

When he returns home, des Esseintes examines his library, which is full of books printed at his request using sumptuous materials. He looks through the works of Charles Baudelaire (French poet, 1821-1867) and praises their profundity, subtlety and power. He also reflects on Catholic literature and laments the fact that the impact of eloquent Christian literature has lessened since Jacques-Bénigne Bossuet (French bishop, preacher and writer, 1627-1704). He also criticises contemporary Catholic literature, which he thinks is dominated by crude, pedantic individuals, although he does concede that some Christian authors are interesting. These include Jules Barbey d'Aurevilly (French writer, 1808-1889) and Léon Bloy (French writer, 1846-1917).

CHAPTER XIII

The heat has become overwhelming over the past few days that des Esseintes ventures into his garden for the first time. From there, he can see children fighting, which temporarily distracts him from his mental torment. He reflects on the absurdity of human life and on the fact that good intentions can have harmful consequences. He considers procreation to be folly, given the current state of the world. Once he has gone back inside, he meditates while contemplating an astrolabe (a disk-shaped instrument used for measuring the height of stars above the horizon). After reflecting on his memories, he is overwhelmed by depressing thoughts about manipulative commercialism, which is now the prevailing mindset in society.

CHAPTER XIV

Des Esseintes arranges the few secular works in his library. These include books by Baudelaire, Gustave Flaubert (French writer, 1821-1880), Edmond de Goncourt (French writer, 1822-1896), Zola and Verlaine (French poet, 1844-1896). His favourite authors include Edgar Allan Poe (American writer, 1809-1849), who wrote works of psychological horror, Auguste de Villiers de l'Isle-Adam (French writer, 1838-1889) and Stéphane Mallarmé (French poet, 1842-1898), whom he appreciates for his use of his symbols and because the branch of literature he represents seems likely to die with him.

CHAPTER XV

Des Esseintes is now suffering from auditory hallucinations and recalls the chants he learnt during his schooling with the Jesuits. His stomach troubles prevent him from eating and his condition becomes critical, so he resolves to call a doctor, who administers an enema. He also tells des Esseintes that he must return to Paris and lead a normal life if he wants to get better.

CHAPTER XVI

Des Esseintes is infuriated by the idea that he will have to rejoin society even though his greatest wish is to get away from it, and is convinced that nobody else is capable of understanding him. He wishes that he could find faith, but knows that this is impossible. He reflects bitterly on the rise of the bourgeoisie, the increasing power of money and the mediocrity that now prevails in society. He knows that this is what he is returning to and is aware that his efforts to escape it were futile, which inspires him to offer up a final desperate prayer. The novel closes on a tense note, as des Esseintes is torn between the desire to believe and the impossibility of faith.

CHARACTER STUDY

The exploration of des Esseintes' inner life

Against Nature is centred on des Esseintes' inner life, which means that it does not tell a story made up of a series of events, but rather explores the inner workings of a specific character and their personality. It can be said that nothing happens in the novel apart from the changes in the protagonist's behaviour and thoughts. The events narrated are drawn from his past and are not recounted because they have any inherent narrative value, but rather to shed light on his current thoughts and state of mind.

A turbulent life

Des Esseintes is the last descendent of an old aristocratic family which has been weakened by generations of consanguineous marriages, resulting in "a weakened constitution" and "the effeminisation of the males". Des Esseintes is around 30 years old and has pale skin, cold blue eyes and a pointed blond beard. He became an orphan at the age of 17, and his memories of his parents are mundane and sad. He was solitary and neglected during his childhood before being sent to be educated by the Jesuits. He has positive memories of this time, which also had a decisive influence on his artistic interests.

The time he has spent in different social environments and the debauchery and pleasures he has indulged in have left him disillusioned and exhausted: he is virtually impotent and suffers from stomach ailments and nervous disorders, which have always plagued him but which have been aggravated by his life of excess and his heredity. He suffers from a kind of neurosis which can lead to violent headaches, hallucinations and fainting spells. At the start of the novel, he thinks that he is "ripe for isolation" as he no longer expects anything from life. He therefore moves to a house in the countryside, which he furnishes according to his personal tastes and where he plans to live a reclusive life.

An elitist mindset

Des Esseintes is sophisticated and extremely demanding, which means that he is tired of what he sees as the mediocrity and narrow-mindedness of his contemporaries. Nobody escapes his ire: old bores and attractive young people, aristocrats and ordinary people, and even intellectuals, whom he had hoped would rise above pettiness and materialism, all incur his wrath. He is a misanthropic hypochondriac and feels an acute, sustained sense of suffering when he looks at certain people, as he finds them aesthetically displeasing and considers them an infuriating symbol of mediocrity and disregard for art. For him, art and culture exist in a vacuum, unsullied by the impurities of the real world.

He is captivated by art, and particularly by literature, and carefully selects works that are in line with his tastes. Each time he reads one of his favourite books he becomes a little more critical and ends up turning away from the works that helped to hone his critical tendencies by intensifying his unusual ideas and desires, which are increasingly at odds with the prevailing conventions:

- Like Émile Zola, he initially believes that the artist's temperament is the only thing that counts, but he eventually comes to the conclusion that only his own temperament and those that are similar to it are valid.
- He is a lover of imagination and artifice: he lives for sensations that stimulate his imagination and uses decoration, scents, tastes and reading to feel as though he is travelling. He believes that humans are capable of reproducing all the delights of nature and even inventing new ones. For example, when he is reflecting on decorative plants, he thinks "that in a few years man can bring about a choice that indolent nature would take centuries to produce". However, his elitism means that he disdains industry, as it is practised by the majority of ordinary people.
- He sees artistic links between the five senses and experiences synaesthesia: "the taste of each liqueur corresponded, in his way of thinking, to the sound of an instrument. Dry curaçao, for example, to the clarinet, the song of which is both tart and velvety […]".
- The works he enjoys the most are those which mark the end of an era, as he believes that they

contain decadence, subtlety, the swansong of a dying sensibility and a desire to say everything that has remained unsaid until now.

- Finally, he only sees works as pure if they have caused controversy and are scorned by the general public, finding favour with only a small elite. Once a work becomes too popular and is accepted and admired even by people he considers foolish, he begins to hate it and sees flaws that were never apparent to him before.

Endless suffering?

In the end, the solitude he previously craved and his withdrawal from the tumult and mediocrity of society only lead to distress and neurosis. He withdraws into his own world until his mind is "saturated with literature and art" and the mundane memories he was trying to repress resurface in spite of his efforts to forget them. His declining health and his doctor's advice eventually force him to return to a society that he has nothing but contempt for, and where he has no more hope of finding peace than he did in isolation.

ANALYSIS

The preposition "against" (represented in the original French title by the adverbial construction "À rebours", meaning "backwards" or "in reverse") reflects Husymans' desire to confound his readers' expectations. He initially planned to call his novel *Seul* ("Alone") as a way of emphasising des Esseintes' progressive intellectual and spatial withdrawal, but the final title indicates a broader objective, namely that of challenging the conventions of the contemporary novel.

Against Nature defies traditional literary conventions in a number of ways:

- **The language used is complex.** Huysmans rejects simple, familiar, everyday language in favour of artificial, sophisticated, abstruse language that reflects the character he has created. In the original French text, there are loan words (including, for example, terms drawn from the Flemish dialect spoken in Antwerp), rare or archaic words and language that was elaborate and sophisticated even by the standards of the intellectuals of the time, with the aim of appealing to readers with similar intellectual leanings.

- **There is no overall plot.** Rather than a coherent, linear narrative thread, there are numerous short standalone episodes, such as that of the death of the tortoise. The novel can therefore be described as a *roman à tiroirs* ("novel with drawers"), meaning a novel in which the main story is interrupted by secondary narratives, which may themselves be interrupted by other stories. Indeed, the continual interruption of the narrative means that the only thing that really advances is the protagonist's neurosis.

- **Huysmans plays with time.** There is no indication of the time the novel is set or any clear, precise chronology, and its structure is disturbed and fragmented through flashbacks, lists, des Esseintes' views on art and narrative and descriptive passages which intermingle and interrupt one another without any coherent logic. Numerous lengthy digressions replace the episodes which would constitute the action of a traditional novel.

- **He also plays with the characteristics of different literary genres.** The novel features elements typically associated with essays, art criticism, prose poetry, monologues and satire, among others, which confounds the reader's expectations. Des Esseintes discusses his ideas, memories, worries and dreams seemingly at random, for example when he talks about Catholic literature (Chapter XII), contemporary literature (Chapter III) and music (Chapter XV).
- **The novel focuses on the main character's inner life.** It defies the expectations of 19th-century readers by placing the focus on des Esseintes' inner life rather than on narrative. It uses small details as the starting point for his thoughts, meditations and mental associations, which are recounted using a mixture of direct and indirect style. In contrast to naturalist writers, who sought to analyse society and the real world, des Esseintes engages in extensive self-examination.
- **Its only protagonist, des Esseintes, can be considered an antihero** due to his undisguised misanthropy and elitism. His behaviour and tastes are atypical:

- he prefers marginal, controversial and widely misunderstood authors such as Baudelaire, Mallarmé and Verlaine, or lesser-known works by respected authors;
- his sexuality could be described as abnormal by the standards of the time, as he experiences same-sex attraction and is virtually impotent;
- he appreciates artificiality, difficulty, the unusual, refinement and decadence;
- he prizes aesthetics in all areas of his life, which marks him out as something of a dandy.

A DANDY ADRIFT

Dandyism

A dandy can be described as "a man who thinks a great deal about his appearance and always dresses in smart clothes" (*Collins English Dictionary*). The main characteristics of dandyism are:

- the use of material elegance to obtain social recognition;
- a desire to distinguish oneself from the masses and push refinement to its limits;

- a predilection for certain items of clothing, such as top hats, canes, ruffled garments and gloves;
- a dignified, haughty, condescending attitude.

In France, the term "dandy" acquired a particular meaning in the mid-19th century, as it came to be used to refer to a person whose refinement signalled their nonconformism and rejection of social conventions and middle-class morality. Whereas dandyism was initially based on external material signifiers, in France after the work of Baudelaire and Villiers de L'Isle-Adam, it came to refer more to a moral attitude which rejected pettiness and vulgarity. Elegance was no longer an end in itself, but now symbolised an inner aristocratic morality, as well as the possible rejection of dominant social values. Des Esseintes is a radical example of this trend, and was reportedly inspired by the famous mid-19th-century dandy Robert de Montesquiou (French writer and critic, 1855-1921).

A declining dandy

In *Against Nature*, des Esseintes is driven by the desire to differentiate himself from other people.

He belongs to an aristocratic family that has lost its former grandeur, views other people with contempt and sees them as vulgar, and spends his time alone, seeking out strong sensations which take a heavy toll on his physical and mental health.

He flees society, fed up with its "puerile and outmoded displays", leading to isolation and the lassitude that results from having already tried everything that life can offer a man of his standing. Consequently, he is left in a state of profound boredom.

Inevitable boredom

References to des Esseintes' "boredom" abound throughout *Against Nature*. This boredom results from his insatiable desire for novelty and new sensations, which are hard to come by, as he views the world around him as bland and insipid. He is constantly pushing limits and becomes increasingly eccentric as time goes on, as can be seen in the episode with the tortoise. He ends up becoming a prisoner of his own refinement and hides behind an artificial mask, in sophisticated but stifling solitude.

A symbol of the Decadent Movement

Des Esseintes' suffering echoes the ideas of the Decadent Movement, which emerged in the late 19th century. The artists linked to this movement, including Barbey d'Aurevilley, Villiers de l'Isle-Adam and Huysmans, felt disgusted with the world around them and had abandoned any belief in aesthetic harmony, instead embracing artifice and perversity. They saw art as a way of discovering new sensations even if this meant flouting contemporary moral codes. *Against Nature* embodies the spirit of the Decadent Movement through its main character, who feels a deep-seated sense of unease and unhappiness, and temporarily finds salvation through art and intense experiences. He also uses books and the perfumes he creates as a way of escaping from his contemporaries. However, even art is not a lasting solution, as after its effects have worn off his boredom and desire for novelty come back and are even more intense than before. He aspires to an aesthetic ideal which is always just out of reach, which leaves him perennially dissatisfied. By the end of the novel, he is completely adrift and feels that his life is utterly meaningless, which drives him to seek absolution in religion.

Faith as a potential solution

Des Esseintes' endless quest for refinement leaves him exhausted and alone, and he turns to religion to keep him from tipping over the edge. In a way, he is like a monk in his withdrawal from the world, but unlike monks, he cannot make himself believe and views religion as a "magnificent imposture". His attempts to believe are really just wishful thinking, and his innate scepticism always wins out in the end. His declining physical and mental health forces him to return to society, where he plans to look for someone who can understand him. However, both the aristocracy and the Church inspire nothing but disgust in him.

Des Esseintes finds himself in a double bind: he is incapable of living in harmony with other people, but he also finds it impossible to completely abandon society. He feels adrift, weary and isolated, and is relying on a miracle to make his way out of his current situation. This is why he prays, becoming a "sceptic who wants to believe". At the end of the novel, he finds himself at an impasse, as he is desperate for salvation but knows that it will not be forthcoming.

There are numerous similarities between des Esseintes and Huysmans' spiritual journeys:

- Before his conversion, Huysmans reflected on the border between interiority and exteriority. This reflection can be seen in des Esseintes' withdrawal from society.
- Huysmans' contempt for excessively prudish or ignorant people echoes des Esseintes' rejection of those he considers mediocre or overly pious.
- Like des Esseintes, who was taught by Jesuits and has read a great deal of Catholic literature, Huysmans claimed to have "studied" the Church in the course of his writing.
- Both the author and his creation experience metaphysical uncertainty. According to Barbey d'Aurevilly, Huysmans even found himself torn between suicide and religious conversion, eventually opting for the latter.
- In the preface to the novel, Huysmans acknowledges that religion has the power to cure: it "explains origins and causes, points out conclusions, offers remedies". This is linked to des Esseintes' efforts to get out of his predicament through faith.

A desire to break the rules

Naturalism, which was the dominant literary movement when *Against Nature* was written, advocated faithfully reproducing reality and believed that characters were shaped by elements such as their race, environment and heredity. The preferred subjects of naturalist writers were ordinary, often poor, people. At the start of his career, Huysmans was a follower of Zola, the figurehead of naturalism, but as time went on he came to feel that the movement had stalled and set out to broaden his approach and appeal to more demanding readers who admired more sophisticated, less mainstream authors such as Stéphane Mallarmé. Going beyond the rules of naturalism also enabled him to assert his own identity as a writer and avoid being seen as a pale imitation of Zola.

Enduring naturalist influences

However, Huysmans did not make a clean break with naturalism, and traces of the movement's influence can still be seen in *Against Nature*:

- The beginning of the novel is typical of naturalism, as it outlines the ancestors, psychological makeup and nervous temperament of its protagonist. These elements are referred to again throughout the novel to explain des Esseintes' physical or mental state.
- When he was preparing to write the novel, Huysmans carried out the kind of meticulous documentary research that is typical of naturalism. He catalogued precious stones, flowers and relatively unknown works of literature, and based his descriptions of des Esseintes' neurosis and boredom on contemporary scientific studies. This means that his boredom is presented as an illness rather than merely a kind of malaise.

Criticism of naturalism in *Against Nature*

However, the novel also features a number of direct attacks on naturalism, which are generally expressed through the protagonist:

- He rejects the "vulgar reality of things", preferring imagination and artifice instead, in direct contrast to the naturalist view of science and nature.

- Both his birth and his aspirations mark him out as an aristocrat. He sees ordinary people as mediocre and wants to stay as far away from them as possible, in contrast to naturalists, who mix with their subjects and are meticulous and unflinching in their observation of reality.
- He views the world around him with contempt and is disgusted by its materialism (which goes hand in hand with enthusiasm for progress and positivism). He tries to escape the time he is living in through literature and art and return to a lost, timeless ideal. By contrast, naturalists were firm believers in progress.
- Finally, many of his personality traits are exaggerated and improbable, which contravenes the principles of naturalism.

CRITICAL RECEPTION

Huysmans' desire to break with convention enabled him to stand out from other authors and attract readers' attention. He was expecting the work to receive a frosty reception, so it came as a surprise to him when the public response to it was largely favourable. It was widely praised and critics were generally enthusiastic, although it did not enjoy a large print run (indeed, even today, in spite of its literary importance, *Against Nature* is not a bestseller). The novel responded to a nascent desire for change, and writers such as Barbey d'Aurevilly and Bloy, both of whom are favourites of des Esseintes, saw it as a clear rejection of Zola and his naturalist movement, as well as an indication of the failure of a materialist society.

FURTHER REFLECTION

SOME QUESTIONS TO THINK ABOUT...

- Huysmans' initial title for the novel was *Alone*. Why do you think he opted for *Against Nature* in the end?
- Comment on Huysmans' use of language in the novel.
- At the start of his career, Huysmans was a follower of Zola and the naturalist movement. Can any traces of this be seen in *Against Nature*? Explain your answer.
- In what ways does des Esseintes' behaviour constitute both a voluntary and an involuntary flight from society?
- What do you think that the tortoise with the bejewelled shell is a metaphor for? Develop your answer.
- How would you explain des Esseintes' admiration for Poe and Baudelaire?
- According to des Esseintes' conception of aesthetics, what are the potential links between

art and religion?

- Compare the character of des Esseintes to the dandies Dorian Gray and Lord Henry Wotton in *The Picture of Dorian Gray* (1891) by Oscar Wilde (Irish writer, 1854-1900).
- What place does faith really have in des Esseintes' life? Why does he sometimes feel the need to believe?
- Fragmentation and the exploration of characters' inner lives are two of the defining features of modernist literature from the early 20th century onwards. Give examples of works that became famous thanks to their use of these techniques, and compare their approach to that of *Against Nature*.

We want to hear from you!
Leave a comment on your online library
and share your favourite books on social media!

FURTHER READING

REFERENCE EDITION

- Huysmans, J-K. (2008) *Against Nature*. Trans. King, B. Sawtry: Dedalus.

REFERENCE STUDIES

- Court-Pérez, F. (1987) *Joris-Karl Huysmans*. À rebours. Paris: PUF.

- (No date) Dandy. *Trésor de la langue française*. [Online]. [Accessed 1 August 2018]. Available from: <https://www.le-tresor-de-la-langue.fr/definition/dandy#top>

- (No date) Dandysme. *Trésor de la langue française*. [Online]. [Accessed 1 August 2018]. Available from: <https://www.le-tresor-de-la-langue.fr/definition/dandysme#top>

- Grojnowski, D. (1998) Le sujet d'*À rebours*. *Romantisme*. 102.

- Jourde, P. (1991) *Huysmans :* À rebours. *L'identité impossible*. Paris: Champion.

- Millet, D. (1996) Preface and notes to *En Route* by Joris-Karl Huysmans. Paris: Gallimard.

- Rey, A. (1998) *Dictionnaire historique de la langue française*. Vol I. Paris: Le Robert.

- Smeets, M. (2003) *Huysmans l'inchangé : histoire d'une conversion*. Amsterdam: Rodopi.

MORE FROM BRIGHTSUMMARIES.COM

- Reading guide – *Là-bas* by Joris-Karl Huysmans.

Although the editor makes every effort to verify the accuracy of the information published, BrightSummaries.com accepts no responsibility for the content of this book.

www.brightsummaries.com

Ebook EAN: 9782808011419

Paperback EAN: 9782808011426

Legal Deposit: D/2018/12603/317

This guide was written with the collaboration of Gilles Clamar for the summary of the Notice and Chapter 12, the character study and the sections "The meaning of the title" and "A dandy adrift".

Cover: © Primento

Digital conception by Primento, the digital partner of publishers.